the
essence
of
style

the essence of CARIBBEAN STYLE

SUZANNE SLESIN, STAFFORD CLIFF,
JACK BERTHELOT, MARTINE GAUMÉ,
DANIEL ROZENSZTROCH
AND GILLES DE CHABANEIX

THAMES AND HUDSON

Thank you again to all the people who allowed us to photograph their homes on the islands represented in Caribbean Style; *to our agent, Barbara Hogenson of the Lucy Kroll Agency; Beth Gardiner, our editorial assistant; Ian Hammond, our art associate; Howard Klein, art director of Clarkson Potter, and Renato Stanisic, designer; Joan Denman and Andrea C. Peabbles; and our editor, Roy Finamore, who made sure that this new* Caribbean Style, *although smaller in size, was just as consistently strong as the original.*

First published in Great Britain in 1994 by Thames and Hudson Ltd, London by arrangement with Clarkson N. Potter, Inc./Publishers, 201 East 50th Street, New York, New York 10022.

Copyright © 1985, 1994 by Suzanne Slesin, Stafford Cliff, Jack Berthelot, Martine Gaumé, Daniel Rozensztroch, and Gilles de Chabaneix.

British Library Cataloguing-in-Publication Data

A catalogue record for this book is available from the British Library.

ISBN 0-500-27804-0

Printed and bound in China.

CONTENTS

INTRODUCTION

The Caribbean. The place immediately brings to mind specific colors, arranged in a specific way. Blue above, blue below. White for the beach, green for the coconut palms. Dominating all, the gold of the sun. This little book will add to that palette the colors and shades of the lives of a people seen through their homes.

All West Indians, whether they live on the Bahamas to the north or the Greater or Lesser Antilles to the south, are the descendants of transplanted peoples. Spaniards lured by dreams of gold were the primary conquerors of the Caribbean. Then, slowly, the English and French began to colonize the Lesser Antilles, which the Spaniards had ignored. From the 1600s until the mid-19th century, millions of enslaved Africans were convoyed to the islands. Others emigrated from far-off Asia. All were forced to reeducate themselves in order to survive. The conditions they met were often unbearable, but out of their struggles and efforts a Creole culture and a Creole way of life were born.

The early settlers built only temporary shelters. They clung to the idea of one day returning to their homelands. But with the development of the sugar trade, permanent homes were constructed. The grandest houses in the Antilles were built with wealth derived from sugarcane. Many of them have completely disappeared or fallen into ruin. Those that remain are fragile relics of a bygone world and are today in danger of disappearing with the death of the sugar trade.

The first characteristics of a truly Caribbean style appeared during the 18th century. But it was only in the following century that a fully coherent, specifically Caribbean architecture developed. Caribbean style represents a vernacular architecture without official agreement or approval. It is not involved with learned concepts and does not frequent the seats of academe. It is a truly living style and is the fruit of experience. The diverse components group themselves as for a painting. Above the thickets, the royal palms, which once provided wood for construction, are evidence of long-gone settlements. The tamarind, which offers restful shade and whose fruit is rich in vitamin C, is planted today, as long ago, between the house and the kitchen—which were traditionally located in different buildings, as a protection against fire.

This book is certain to be a surprise for West Indians themselves. They live on their own islands, in a kind of exile from all the other islands. Each island is considered by its inhabitants a world unto itself, the far-off colony of a Western power. They are not acquainted with one another, and in any case, they believe that what is best in themselves comes from Europe or elsewhere. In these pages, West Indians will discover an undeniable, deep-rooted common Creole heritage.

It is their Creole identity that unites these cultures born in the conquest of the New World and anchored in islands of the Americas. Their wealth is drawn from their diversity.

PRECEDING PAGES: *Rose Hall Great House was built about 5 miles east of Montego Bay in Jamaica between 1770 and 1780.*

PEOPLE OF THE CARIBBEAN

To become familiar with the people of the Caribbean, it is not sufficient merely to enter the homes of the upper classes. Christmas wreaths that last all year, children's balloons, and highly colored prints are just some of the things that enliven the interiors of simple residences—just as the exteriors of the houses are brightened by sharp, lively colors. The houses of the townspeople and peasants, as well the buildings created in the service of colonial powers, have stories to tell.

Jan Morris, the well-known English author, has written that the Caribbean islands "have been variously ruled by the French, the Spaniards, the English, the Dutch, the Danes and the Americans, and some indeed have been passed so repeatedly from sovereignty to sovereignty that they are a positive mish-mash of influences and memories; while the great black majority of the populace, descended from African slaves, have acquired over the generations myriad ethnic strains and symptoms, from the high cheekbones of the original Carib Indians to the commanding postures of European aristocrats."

The architectural style of the Caribbean was developed by borrowing from the different cultures that were in contact throughout the islands. Elements of Creole architecture that can be traced to the colonists include jalousie shutters and the symmetrical composition of façades organized around a central entrance. The French brought dormer windows, and only on the islands colonized by the English is the taste for porches prevalent. The Spanish built houses of very simple forms.

Finally, some characteristics were provided by the black populations who were brought over into slavery. As in Africa, the blacks of the Antilles preferred darkness in the interiors of their cabins and closed them hermetically. This African custom was reinforced by the circumstances of slavery. The slave had nothing that really belonged to him. The interior of his house was the single element of his life over which he had some control.

PRECEDING PAGES: *Students on Marie-Galante, an island that is part of Guadeloupe, study with a semiretired schoolteacher.*

ABOVE: *On Haiti, people live in houses where the roofs and sides are made of royal palms, a building material that was used by the Amerindians.* **LEFT:** *An owner of a house in Grand Fonds, on Guadeloupe, visits with a family friend on the verandah.*

CLOCKWISE FROM TOP LEFT: *A Haitian farmer surveys the expansive view from the small garden near his house. On Haiti, a man is half hidden in a grove of mango trees. Oxen pull a cart on Marie-Galante—a typical Antillean scene. A child stands on the wide stone steps at the rear of the Alexandra Hotel, on Haiti. Another child plays near the rear gallery of a house on Antigua.*

17

On the balcony of an old house in the center of Point-à-Pitre, on Guadeloupe, the children of the family pose near pots of blooming bougainvillea.

Narrow roads on which people travel on foot or by motorbike link villages throughout the Caribbean.

Wooden boats, often outfitted with outboard motors and topped with an elaborate system of fishnets, are a common sight.

ABOVE: *Members of the hotel staff of the Alexandra Hotel on Haiti stand by the entrance to the original kitchen, which is housed in a separate building from the main house.* **LEFT:** *A child peeks out of the window of a pastel house on Nevis.*

The house of a retired school-teacher on Marie-Galante was built by a carpenter for his sister. A craftsman's master-piece, it is considered a fine example of local folk art.

ABOVE: *A bus, with its rooftop load, makes its way through a crowded Haitian marketplace.* **RIGHT:** *A man stands on the steps of a small shingled house on Nevis. Its twin peaks are a typical architectural detail on the English-speaking islands.*

ABOVE: *Friends and family swim in the river that runs behind a house in the hills of Guadeloupe.* **RIGHT:** *Some of the inhabitants of Nevis swim in a sheltered cove.*

LOOKING OUTSIDE

THE architecture of the Caribbean is a synthesis of different influences. Each island brings to it a unique personality. To the attentive viewer, each island has intrinsic characteristics that distinguish it from the others. As proof of this, it suffices to note the numerous differences between the houses of Guadeloupe and those of Martinique, particularly in the foundations and the rhythms of the façades. And yet these islands have parallel histories. They were colonized by the same nation and the same ethnic groups settled on them. On each island, the same mixture produced different effects and assumed different qualities.

The architectural style developed at the same time as a lifestyle that was specifically Caribbean. The architecture of the Caribbean is first and foremost an architecture for life out-of-doors. Daily activities take place in spaces that are mostly outside the framework of the house itself. And even the framework is open to the outdoors, offering protection only from the sun and the rain.

In the Antilles, houses are sited and domestic activities planned so as to take advantage of the dominant trade *winds—winds that blow constantly from the east to the west, bringing with them a freshness that is indispensable to life on the islands.*

In hot climates, there are many hours when it is more pleasant to be outside than inside. Buildings become a background canvas for a composition in which the garden is as precisely laid out as the house itself. Between these two areas—extra muros and intra muros—the gallery is an organic link, interior and exterior at the same time.

Neither an indoor nor an outdoor space, the gallery or verandah provides a separation between the brightness and heat of the outside world and the coolness and modulated light of the interior. It is not surprising that it is the decorative showplace of the house, an element to be experienced and appreciated from both the exterior and the interior, no matter what the scale of the house to which it belongs.

PRECEDING PAGES: *On St. Barth's, a garden in the popular taste features a pair of cacti in white-polka-dotted pots, a delicate wrought-iron gate, and an arch covered in bougainvillea.*

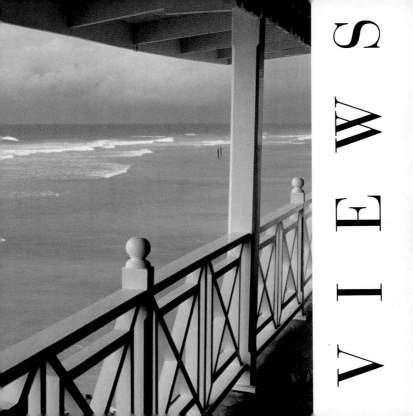

VIEWS

PRECEDING PAGES: *On Barbados, a terrace provides an uninterrupted view of the ocean as well as a space that is protected from the sun.* **RIGHT:** *A forest of coconut trees separates a house on Nevis from the sea.*

In a valley on Antigua, village houses are nestled in the lush green countryside.

The method of agriculture follows the terrain of the islands. Stone fences delineate the fields on St. Barthélémy.

The view from Clarence House, an official residence for the government of Antigua, is of English Harbour, the former British naval base in the Lesser Antilles.

ABOVE: *A row of coconut palms lines one of the canals on the Waterworks estate, on Montserrat.* **RIGHT:** *Nestled among palm trees, situated by the water, or set atop a hill, the Caribbean house is an intrinsic part of the varied landscape.*

ABOVE: *Small houses are set at the bottom of the hill under a turbulent sky.* **LEFT:** *An abandoned windmill in Les Grands Fonds de Ste. Anne on Guadeloupe is a romantic sight.*

A sweeping verandah on Nevis overlooks a lush garden.

ABOVE: *Sugarcane is cut by hand on the gentle slopes near the sea on Martinique.* **LEFT:** *Sea and land are visually tied together in many of the Caribbean islands.* **OVERLEAF:** *Le Diamant, an enormous rock off the coast, is one of Martinique's landmarks.*

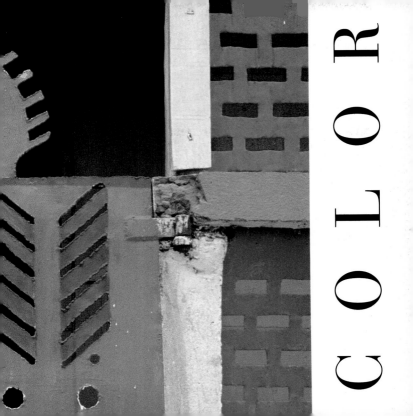

COLOR

ABOVE AND RIGHT: *Hot pink, bright yellow, vibrant turquoise, and luminescent lilac are some of the colors of island buildings.*
PRECEDING PAGES: *On Guadeloupe, the bright colors and decorative sunrise motifs create a naive tableau.*

A house on Haiti provides a striking example of the strong and uninhibited graphic designs that are typical of many houses on the island.

ABOVE: *The lacelike delicacy of the balcony railing and the panel over the door contrast the bright blue trim of a Port-au-Prince residence.* **LEFT:** *The yellow-and-red shutters are a counterpoint to the blue walls of this house on Montserrat.* **OVERLEAF:** *Yellow, blue, and red are the palette of this Haitian country house.*

RIGHT: *Shocking pink and pale yellow offer an unusual color combination.* **BELOW:** *The red designs in relief on the verandah gate add a jaunty note to a blue-and-white painted house.*

ABOVE: *Green paint outlines the roof, windows, shutters, and doors of a bright yellow house.*
RIGHT: *The reinforced-concrete walls and corrugated tin roof have been painted in compatible blues and greens.*

Vibrant turquoise with a moss-green trim was chosen for this triple-peaked-roof town house.

The round louvered window below the peak of a pink painted house on Haiti lets air into the attic.

66

On Haiti, a two-tone pink-and-blue house, with a roof decorated in fretwork, stands as a piece of folk art in a barren landscape.

FAÇADES

ABOVE: *Tall breadfruit trees, part of the long-established garden, frame the entrance to Pécoul, a 1760 sugarcane plantation house on Martinique. The matching openings of the front and back windows allow views through the main building.* **PRECEDING PAGES:** *Pécoul presents a symmetrical façade that is broken only by the kitchen chimney at right.*

ABOVE: *Zevalos, a tall and elegant building made of prefabricated cast-iron units, rises above the flatlands of Grande-Terre on the island of Guadeloupe.* **RIGHT:** *The use of brick and the wrought-iron balconies of a house in Pointe-à-Pitre are rare on Guadeloupe.*

ABOVE: *The extravagantly peaked roof of a house on Haiti is an example of the fancifulness that is characteristic of many of the structures on the island.*

BELOW: *A profusion of crotons is near the former vegetable garden at the side of Pécoul, on Martinique. A huge stone urn stands on the lawn.* **OVERLEAF:** *La Frégate, with its second floor above the gallery, is typical of Martinican plantation houses.*

The gallery at the Villa Nova Great House on Barbados has crisp white latticework over-grown with plants.

Trellis-shuttered windows are set in the wood-shingled wall of the 1740 L'Hermitage, one of the oldest wooden houses in the Antilles.

*In a house in Reading on the island of Jamaica, tall louvered
bedroom doors open directly onto the back garden.*

Arched windows and curved shutters ornament one of the sides of the Alexandra Hotel in Jacmel, Haiti.

Open or enclosed, made of prefabricated metal or artisan-carved wood, a variety of balconies and verandahs decorate the city and country houses of Montserrat, Guadeloupe, Antigua, and Haiti.

ABOVE: *The fanciful fretwork and curved balconies of a private house on Haiti are a new interpretation of the original turn-of-the-century Victorian detailing.* **LEFT:** *Plants in pots punctuate the verandah of Bois Debout, a plantation house on Guadeloupe.*

ABOVE: *A delicate cornice decorates a small corrugated tin–roofed house.* **RIGHT:** *A wood balcony faces the rear courtyard of Maison Nemausat, in Basse-Terre, Guadeloupe.*

ABOVE: *Each of the small buildings that make up a vacation compound on St. Barth's is topped with a red corrugated-metal roof and trimmed in a decorative border.* **LEFT:** *Set on a hill, the main house of La Pagésie, at Pointe Noire on Guadeloupe, is surrounded by groves of coffee trees.*

The verandah's cutout wood motifs in the shape of fish heads are characteristic on Marie-Galante, an island of fishermen. The sunrise motif is for good luck.

The white-and-pastel-walled 18th-century houses in San Juan, Puerto Rico, feature wood and wrought-iron cantilevered balconies that give the buildings their Spanish look.

*A simple wooden bench,
painted to match the shutters,
stands on the rear gallery of
Waterworks, a plantation
house on Montserrat.*

ABOVE: *In Pointe-à-Pitre, Guadeloupe, wrought-iron balconies decorate the shuttered windows of a city house.* **RIGHT:** *Tall trees shade the front façade of a small inn above Plymouth, on Montserrat, that was a family residence at the turn of the century.*

GARDENS

PRECEDING PAGES: *In a late-19th-century house in Basse-Terre, on Guadeloupe, the ground-floor gallery is planted with large ferns in terra-cotta pots.*
RIGHT: *Pink flowers provide a touch of color in a garden on Guadeloupe.*

The plants and flowers on the different tropical islands—including lychee trees, **ABOVE RIGHT,** *and huge water lilies,* **ABOVE FAR RIGHT—** *are as colorful as they are lush.*

ABOVE: *The irrigation reservoirs at Bois Debout, an estate located at Basse-Terre on Guadeloupe, were designed to be aesthetic as well as functional.* **LEFT:** *Red draceana bushes frame a shimmering cascade on the grounds of a sugarcane estate known as Pécoul on Martinique.*

An orchid nursery is in back
of the garden that surrounds
the Villa Nova Great House on
Barbados.

Large terra-cotta jars that were the ballast on cargo ships transporting meat and oil from Europe to the Lesser Antilles, as

108

well as garden ornaments made of terra-cotta, now decorate many Caribbean gardens and gateways.

RIGHT: *An old marble bathtub has been planted with water lilies.* **BELOW AND TOP FAR RIGHT:** *Spectacular pink blossoms and giant crotons are some of the striking features of a garden on Martinique.*

110

LEFT: *Curved stone benches are set among the trees as a shady resting spot in a garden on Barbados.*

The pale colors of the trim complement the luxuriant garden.

In the Caribbean, trees are always green, and only a few flowers and fruits have distinct seasons. An asparagus fern has grown to gigantic proportions, **ABOVE RIGHT.**

The traveler's-tree, **ABOVE LEFT,** *collects water at the base of its leaves; the waterwheel that stands at the end of the canal on an estate on Guadeloupe adds a picturesque touch,* **ABOVE RIGHT.**

Because the plantation house
of Beauséjour is situated on
the north coast of Martinique,
which is the most humid part
of the island, the garden
surrounding the house is
particularly luxuriant.

On Nevis, the garden of the
Montpelier estate, an old
plantation house that is now
a hotel, offers a play of light
and shade. Huge specimens
of ficus grow over the wide
steps of volcanic stone.

*A small corner of a garden on
Martinique is used as a nursery
for potted orchids.*

Huge bushes with vibrantly colored flowers grow near the main house of an estate on Guadeloupe.

Vacation houses on St. Barth's are linked by planked walkways lined with plants.

LOOKING INSIDE

TODAY'S West Indian houses are amalgams of scholarly architecture on the one hand and on the other the architecture of the countrysides of both Europe and Africa. Thus within one luxurious house can be found windows ordered in a totally Palladian manner and doors closed with wooden latches based on African designs.

The house and its surroundings, the furniture, and the garden reflect the Caribbean sensibility and the order of society. Thus the expressly desired discomfort of the sofa on which one sits while waiting to be received by the master of the house; the whispers and mumbling voices that can be heard through thin wooden partitions; the sensuality of exotic veined woods, richly scented, warm in tone. All are part of a decor that hides and reveals at the same time— the shutters that shield an inquisitive stare; the row of doors that let in light and that sometimes frame a momentary scene uncovered in passing.

Perhaps in memory of the slave whose cabin was a refuge for privacy, West Indians declare their love for their homes with the delicate frills and lacework that adorn *galleries and interiors. Large plantation houses, the most imposing residences in the Antilles, are set on the highest ground, from which they dominate the landscape and profit from the winds. In the 18th century, galleries and verandahs suitable to the climate gave the great European-inspired houses an essential Creole characteristic.*

In the towns, which are hot and sheltered from the wind, the typical house sits on a narrow street and usually includes a store or warehouse on the street level.

The popular Caribbean house, or case, *is usually a rural dwelling. For many Antilleans who have traditionally owned little else, the house is the object of a special affection. That explains the care and attention lavished on these modest buildings, from the imagination shown in each uniquely decorated exterior to the pride reflected in the well-arranged furniture and mementos inside.*

PRECEDING PAGES: *A wood composition depicting a bowl filled with fruit has been cut out and applied to the paneled wall of a dining room on Jamaica.*

LIVING

ABOVE: *Louvered panels are used as interior partitions to divide the sitting room on the estate of Good Hope on Jamaica.*
PRECEDING PAGES: *At Parham Hill, a plantation house on Antigua, the plank wood floor in the office, where workers came to collect their wages, has been stained red to match the walls.*

BELOW: *A barometer hangs on the wall of the formal living room of the Good Hope Great House. A large dog lies on the cool floor that has been polished to a mirrorlike finish.*

RIGHT: *In the sitting room of Le Maud'Huy, an 1873 plantation house on the east coast of Guadeloupe, two rocking chairs are pulled up to a small table on which are displayed bottles filled with the customary rum punch.*
OVERLEAF: *The spacious gallery at La Frégate on Martinique has been furnished with comfortable chairs and functions as a living room.*

*Pécoul, on Martinique, is
an estate that has remained
in the same family since its
beginnings in the mid-18th
century. Ancestral portraits
welcome visitors to the house.*

ABOVE: *The rocking chair on a tiled porch on Guadeloupe provides a shady and inviting place to enjoy the cool evening air.* **RIGHT:** *The rocking chairs and a small table in the living room of a suburban house in St. Claude, on Guadeloupe, were crafted in the Caribbean. An antique gramophone is positioned in the corner by the door.*

A carved wood panel that illustrates an underwater scene covers one wall in the dining room of a vacation house on Jamaica.

140

The louvered living room window is draped with green cotton. Shiny ceramic tile covers the floor.

The wall sconce in a Jamaican dining room has been carved in a pineapple motif.

An imitation bamboo storage unit with pull-out wicker drawers and bronze-colored hardware stands in front of a bedroom window on Jamaica. Frangipani blossoms fill a green vase.

Three arches bisect the living room of Parham Hill, a 1722 plantation house on Antigua. The ornate architectural details, painted in white, contrast with the dark green of the walls.

RIGHT: *The walls, floor, and furniture in the living room at Waterworks, a plantation house on Montserrat, are all of dark wood.* **OVERLEAF:** *The front gallery of the 1760 plantation house known as Pécoul, on Martinique, functions as a living room. The ocher and turquoise hues, which are reminiscent of 18th-century French interiors, contrast with the softer variegated colors of the tile floor.*

150

LEFT AND BELOW: *Brass chandeliers hang from the high ceiling in the formal sitting room of a house in Port-au-Prince, Haiti. A series of arched doorways acts as a partition between the main reception rooms.* **OVERLEAF:** *In Basse-Terre, Guadeloupe, the living room of an antiques-filled house takes up the entire ground floor.*

154

In the main living room of Clarence House, an official residence on Antigua, a portrait of Queen Elizabeth and Prince Philip hangs between two windows and above a desk and chair.

155

ABOVE LEFT: *The soft turquoise frame of the Haitian rocking chair harmonizes with the early-20th-century tile floor.* **ABOVE RIGHT:** *In the hall of a converted town house in Jacmel, Haiti, hangs a contemporary pen-and-ink sketch of the façade of the hotel.*

156

ABOVE LEFT: *A few hats, a bag, an umbrella, and canes hang on a rack in the gallery of a house on Guadeloupe.* **ABOVE RIGHT:** *A high-legged mahogany console, one of the rare pieces of furniture that are of pure Martinican origin, was designed as a stand-up desk.*

An assortment of typically
Caribbean rockers furnishes
the living room of Le Maud'
Huy, a plantation house on
Guadeloupe that was built in
1873 by August Pauvert, the
director of the sugarcane
factory in a nearby village.

In a house known as L'Hermitage, on the island of Nevis, a water-color hangs in the corner of the ground-floor bedroom; an oil lamp recalls the time when the house lacked electricity; mangoes sit on

160

*the verandah table; and dried pieces of coral are displayed on a
stand that was used for holding water jars.*

RIGHT: *The main sitting room in one of the oldest houses in the Caribbean, the mid-17th-century St. Nicholas Abbey on Barbados, has been furnished with a variety of rockers and chairs.* **OVERLEAF:** *At the bottom of the mahogany staircase at Le Maud'Huy on Guadeloupe stands a planter's chair. The master of the house would rest his legs on the long swing-out arms while a servant removed his boots.*

163

ABOVE: *Antique dolls occupy some of the chairs in the brilliant blue living room at the Alexandra Hotel on Haiti.* **RIGHT:** *At the entrance to the covered gallery at La Frégate, on Martinique, rustic chairs recall the feeling of a French country house.*

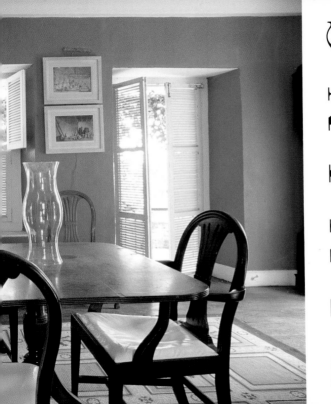

DINING

170

ABOVE: *A doorway frames the view into the formal dining room of the 1750 Governor's House on Montserrat.* **LEFT:** *At the rear of a house in Port-au-Prince, Haiti, two doorways separate the dining room from the terrace. On the table is a bouquet of anthurium.* **PRECEDING PAGES:** *Glass hurricane lamps stand on the dining table at Parham Hill on Antigua. The vermilion-colored walls add to the elegance of the room.*

In St. Nicholas Abbey on
Barbados, the formal dining
room has been situated to
receive the afternoon sun.
The walls are paneled.

ABOVE LEFT AND ABOVE RIGHT: *Crystal glasses and silver serving pieces sparkle on a rolling cart in the green-walled dining room at Water-works, on Montserrat.*

ABOVE LEFT: *The intimate family dining room at La Frégate, on Martinique, is furnished with white painted furniture.* **ABOVE RIGHT:** *The butterfly-shaped chair backs in a popular house at Anse Bertrand on Guadeloupe are the local artisan's signature.*

LEFT: *At L'Hermitage, a 1740 wood-shingled house on Nevis, the combination living and dining room is situated in the oldest part of the house.*
OVERLEAF: *The informal dining room of the Good Hope Great House has been furnished with English-style mahogany furniture hand-crafted on Jamaica.*

180

At Pécoul, on Martinique, the
centrally placed main room
of the house is used for dining.
The mahogany dining table
and console contrast with the
unglazed tile floors, red slat-
back chairs, and yellow walls.

The formal dining room at Le Maud'Huy, on Guadeloupe, features a huge oval table of polished mahogany. Hurricane lamps replace the more usual candlesticks.

ABOVE: *A system of screenlike louvered partitions stands at one end of the large dining room of Antigua's Weatherhills estate.* **LEFT:** *A wall-hung china rack holds a collection of flea-market finds in the green-walled dining room of Maison Nemausat, on Guadeloupe.*

RIGHT: *The space that functions as the main living area in a popular house in Grand Fonds, on Martinique, has been painted pink and green.* **BELOW:** *At Pécoul, on Martinique, the mahogany dining table is surrounded by red slat-backed chairs. The floor is unglazed tile.*

The wood plank walls of the dining room of the Charlotte Inn, in Lucea on the north coast of Jamaica, have been painted royal blue. A mahogany console stands against one wall. The tables are surrounded by English Chippendale-style chairs.

SLEEPING

ABOVE AND RIGHT: *The carved mahogany pineapple and twisted rope detailing on the four-poster canopy beds is typically Jamaican.*
PRECEDING PAGES: *The white gauze mosquito netting contributes to the dreamlike quality of a bedroom on St. Barthélémy.*

A chaise with a double shell–shaped base sits under the windows facing the ocean in the master bedroom of the late-18th-century Rose Hall Great House in Jamaica.

*The uprights of the high
four-poster bed in one of the
bedrooms at L'Hermitage, on
Nevis, are thin and graceful.
The stool facilitates climbing
into bed.*

198

ABOVE AND LEFT: *Mahogany is the wood used for the frames and carved posts of many beds in the Caribbean. The mosquito netting and white bedclothes contrast with the dark wood.* **OVERLEAF:** *Yards of mosquito netting hang above the two double four-poster beds at Pécoul, on Martinique.*

199

*One of the bedrooms in the
Charlotte Inn in Lucea,
Jamaica, has an old-fashioned
bathtub in the room, merely
partitioned off with a plastic
lace-patterned curtain.*

ABOVE LEFT: *An iron bed and a chest for a baby's layette furnish a bedroom on Guadeloupe.* **ABOVE RIGHT:** *The mahogany bed is a Guadaloupian variation of the standard four-poster.*

ABOVE LEFT: *The pale green color scheme contributes to the serenity of the bedroom on Antigua.* **ABOVE RIGHT:** *Mosquito netting is tied above an iron bed in a blue-walled bedroom on Guadeloupe.*

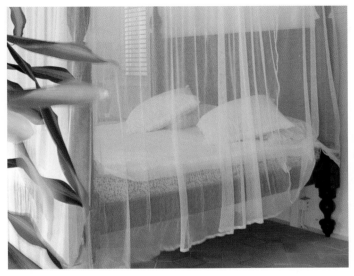

ABOVE: *A four-poster bed swathed in mosquito netting is in a simply furnished St. Barth's guest room.* **LEFT:** *One of the bedrooms in St. Nicholas Abbey is furnished with an ornate 19th-century English bed.*

Other titles in the series